W

MW01140769

Suzanne Jubb has not only honored her father with his simple, straightforward advice but acknowledged his commitment to assist his children to be independent and self-reliant. Lovingly, Suzanne shares the lessons in a way that adolescents and adults can benefit. No matter your country or your currency the lessons are universal. This is a book to share with your loved ones.

Peggy Morrison-Thurston Director, Dropout Prevention/Alternative Education Broward County Public Schools Fort Lauderdale, Florida

This book is extremely helpful and easy to understand. It offers you a very basic guideline to get you started on your journey to financial freedom. It's the stuff that gets you out of bed in the morning because you are committed to improving your life and the lives of those around you. Let the author motivate you to start building your Golden Goose today.

Linda Healing
Author, *Regaining your Passion*

Suzanne Jubb's "The Golden Goose" is a simple, easy to read guide to sensible financial management. The objective is to be financially independent and this is clearly laid out with specific steps and guidelines. You will find this book well worthwhile for your personal benefit and I am sure you will want to share it with friends and family so they too can gain its financial wisdom.

Glen E Klassen
Author, Speaker, Chartered Accountant

It is evident in The Golden Goose that the author knows what she values and lives accordingly. Her writing is clearly understood. I wish I had read this financial plan early in my life. She shares what was handed down from her father, a man who saw the money needs of his future and stayed the course, even during lean times. The Golden Goose should also be a mandatory read in the school system to help students develop financial literacy. Suzanne aptly writes how so many of us have money worries and that the pursuit of our dreams are often held back by inadequate funds. She also acknowledges the simple things in life and having a balance. All in all, a motivational, fun, informative read.

Brian Lukyn
Author of "The Un-Retirement Guide™"

Suzanne is not only a gifted writer, she is an amazing teacher. This is evident as she unpacks what is usually a tough subject for so many of us, and makes it simple and easy to understand. One thing I love is that this real life application is good for the young all the way to the young at heart. I think we should have a stack of them in our car and give them as gifts where ever we go.

Kathleen D. Mailer,
International Business Evangelist
#1 Best Selling Author (Walking In The Wake of the Holy Spirit; Living An Ordinary Life, With an Extraordinary God), Founder/Facilitator of "A Book Is Never A Book Boot Camp", Editor-In-Chief of Today's Businesswoman Magazine.

Down to earth information delivered in an authentic "keep it real style". Suzanne gives practical, logical steps to make it happen! This book is the most cost-effective knowledge.

Dawn Campbell
Community Facilitator & Educator

A quick read. Good food for thought. Offers some insight on how important it is to plan for your future.

Paulette Clarke, Retired Math Teacher
Co-author of Math Resources

The Golden Goose is easy to read and understand and has a flavor that piques the reader's interest in wanting to keep turning to the next page. Other financial books can be dry in nature and takeaway principles not easily captured. The message in Suzanne's books is portrayed in a manner that is both enjoyable and interesting, not an easy task given that finances are the main focus. This book is not intimidating to the young or older reader. I encourage anyone reading this to add a copy to the shelves of your own loved ones also.

Wayne Reynolds, Entrepreneur and Private Investor

"Suzanne offers practical and easy-to-follow advice in her book, The Golden Goose. Her explanations and examples are clearly written and laid out, making this a must-have resource for anyone, young or old, who is wanting to improve their financial status and save for the future. I have been inspired by reading Suzanne's book!"

Kate Janzen,
Author of *Moving Forward After Betrayal*
Website: www.movingforwardafterbetrayal.com
Email: kate.janzen2015@gmail.com

THE GOLDEN GOOSE

*One Important Step
to Financial Freedom...
second edition*

SUZANNE D. JUBB

THE GOLDEN GOOSE

One Important Step to Financial! Freedom, *2nd* Edition

Copyright 2016 Fournier Books

ISBN 978-0-9809145-3-5

Suzanne D. Jubb

Red Deer, Ab

Canada

info@suzannejubb.com

www.suzannejubb.com

PRINTED IN CANADA

To my loving dad,
who unknowingly inspired
me to write this book.

Thank you for being such a great role model;
you truly led by example.

To my wonderful boys
Jason, Kyle, Derek,
my beautiful daughter and daughters-in-law
Jenn, Erin and Megan
and my adorable
grandsons and granddaughter
Liam, Jesse, Levi, Hunter, Hudson,
Carter, Ryker and Gracie.

May you all learn from Grandpapa's wisdom.

*To know and not to do
is not yet to know.*

Zen saying

TABLE OF CONTENTS

When I was five years old... "My dad knows every-thing."

When I was eight years old... "My dad doesn't exactly know everything."

When I was 14 years old... "Dad, that was in the old days. It doesn't apply now."

When I was in my twenties... "Dad knows about it but he's been around a long time, and I'm young. I'll think about that tomorrow."

When I was in my thirties... "Maybe we should ask Dad what he thinks."

When I was in my forties... "Dad, what's the simplest way to teach about finances?"

Dad's reply:
"That's easy. Put money away every month and never, ever spend it. Start today, start now."

It's what you learn after you know it all that counts.

John Wooten
(UCLA Basketball coach)

PREFACE

The Golden Goose is simple and easy to read. It's for the old, the young and everyone in-between. It can be used to teach, to guide or just to learn. It's about financial freedom.

- Freedom to build a legacy for our loved ones.

- Freedom to live the life we're designed to live.

- Freedom to give and make a difference in this world. It's about setting an example for those we love.

My father is financially free after following the simple philosophy in this book. I was inspired to pass on the wisdom of my father to my four children, who are now young adults.

In chapter one, you will enjoy reading my father's story. He truly is living the life of his dreams. "Every day is Christmas. If I want something I buy it."

The second chapter is a glossary that will help you understand the financial terms used throughout the book.

The middle chapters include a section on the value of time. There are many visual aids to help you measure where you are today and where you have the potential to be, given your age. These chapters will give perspective into what is possible.

As you know, many people live pay cheque to pay cheque (the Joneses). Do you want to keep doing what the Joneses are doing, or do you want to change your approach and get better results?

The last two chapters offer new choices to help you get started. The ideas are abundant, but unless you take action nothing will change. There's no reason for anyone not to get started. The Golden Goose is an awakening, an "Aha!" It's a reminder to act now.

When you begin to put the philosophy of the Golden Goose into action, be prepared for a changed life. My hope is that you will eventually eliminate your financial burdens. I also encourage you to enjoy the journey as you move towards your financial freedom.

Chapter One:

DAD'S STORY: EVERY DAY IS CHRISTMAS

I have a passion for teaching. I also have an interest in getting ahead financially and encouraging my children to do the same. And so, when I was in my forties, I asked my father the question, **"Dad, what's the simplest way to teach about finances?"**

Dad's reply:
"That's easy. Put money away every month and never, ever spend it.   Start today, start now."

Dad's story:

"A person needs to put money aside. At the very beginning, they may not be able to afford a lot, but they could even start with $25 a month. I believe the best place is in a Registered Retirement Savings Plan (RRSP). That will help them save and it's going to be their pension later on. If you have a pension with your current employer that's even more money getting saved. If you start at a young age, that money is going to grow. It'll compound every year. That's the way I did mine.

"I opened an RRSP Guaranteed Investment Certificate (GIC) account. It's very simple to do. You go to the bank and tell them you want to open an RRSP and they get you set up. Bankers have financial advisors. I've been very happy with mine. They will ask you your risk tolerance. You can afford to go a little riskier when you're young but, as you age, you lower your risk. The advisor will explain this to you.

"A few years ago I also opened an RRSP account with mutual funds but they aren't doing so well right now. Nevertheless, I won't touch that money. It will eventually go up.

"Farming was tough in the '60s. I had to get a second job. I started working at a car dealership and that's when I opened my first RRSP. That was in 1968. I was 36 at the time and I would put in $50 per month. I had to budget for it. Later on I figured I could put more in so I went to $75 and then $100. I'd pay myself first. A percentage of my income would go to my RRSP and then I used up the rest for paying bills and spending money. I never, ever missed an RRSP payment.

"I was lucky enough to be making 18% interest in the early '70s. It was high interest then. When I started in 1968, I was at 8% interest, I think, and then it worked up to 18% interest.

"When I left my job at the dealership I would pay lump sums. In the farming business, there are times that you only get one or two payments a year. That is, when you sell the grain. On those occasions I would put in

$1000-$2000 per year. Usually I would talk to my accountant and ask him how much I should put in my RRSP this year in order to save on my taxes. Whatever he would recommend, I would put in. If I had a big year, I would put more in my RRSP. If I had a lean year, I would put less in. If you put $3000 into an RRSP, that's $3000 that you don't pay on taxes that year. You pay tax when you take it out, though. If I pay taxes it's because I'm making money. If you don't pay taxes, you're not making any money.

"If you make 10% interest a year, it takes about seven years to double your money. When I was making 18% interest, it took about four years to double my money. We had a formula to figure that out, but I don't remember the formula (Rule of 72).

"If you want to make a decent living when you retire, it will take at least a million dollars. I accumulated the million dollars. I'm living off the interest and some capital (my initial investment). We have enough money to buy what we want. Every day is Christmas. If I want something I buy it. A lot of people who are retired today still stress about their budget. Don't get me wrong, we don't throw money away, but we also don't stress about money.

"You have to think that you're going to live to be 90 or more. The rule right now is that by the time I'm 90, I have to have all that RRSP money withdrawn. That age may change in the future. I also can't buy RRSPs after the age of 71. As of the age of 71, you have to start pulling money from your RRSP. You have to pull out a certain percentage and that percentage increases over time. Whatever you don't use, you can still reinvest in another account and use it after you're 90. I will put whatever money I don't use into a Non RRSP GIC. I reached a million dollars in my RRSP in the year 2000. I started drawing from my RRSP when I was 70 (though the age was 69 then). I didn't have to touch my RRSP money before then because I had other money. It allowed more time for my RRSP to grow.

"If you have high interest debts, put less in your RRSPs and pay those debts first. There is big interest on credit cards. Credit cards are the worst things there are, if not used properly. When you start paying 10, 20, or 24% interest, that's one-fifth of what you make. And with those credit cards, it's never 18% interest. When they tell you 18% interest, it's usually about 24% interest. You need to read the fine print. It's compound interest working against you.

"Credit cards are good if you use them properly. You must pay off your balance every month. People at Christmas put thousands of dollars on their credit card and it takes them all year to pay that off. That's very bad money management. You need to figure what that credit card is costing you per month.

"Sometimes you can get a deal on your interest rate but, to get the deal, you have to have a good credit rating. That's just the way it should be, the guy with the good credit rating does not pay the same interest as the guy with a bad credit rating. Do you know why? Because the guy with the good credit rating is less of a risk than the guy with the bad credit rating. If you are a lower risk to the bank and you have money, they're willing to drop your cost of borrowing because they want your business.

"I never paid interest on credit cards. I'd pay my credit card off every month because the interest was so high. I made arrangements at the bank that my credit card would be paid monthly.

"I wrote a lot of cheques. I wrote cheques so I would have a record. I always knew where I was at financially. Every month I'd check my accounts and made sure no mistakes were made. The idea is to budget so you know where you're at. If you're spending too much in one place, you'll see that.

"I never paid overdraft charges or anything. When the bank forgot to transfer my money, they charged me overdraft. I called my bank manager and she fixed the problem. They put the money back in my account. If you pay overdraft on a $10 amount, it'll cost you $5. That is 50 percent of your money. A lot of people pay that, you know.

"Stay away from ATM machines that are not part of your bank. That alone costs you $1.50 a transaction. I didn't know that rule existed, but when I got charged for that transaction I never did it again. These are all little things, but these little things add up at the end of the month and take your profit away.

"I try to tell everybody that when your debt is paid, it's like winning a lottery. When the kids are done with school and leave home, it's like winning a bigger lottery. When the kids were home, we never had an extra penny in our pocket. We were always on the last penny. But all of a sudden the kids leave and we have money in our pocket. But, again, we no longer have to dish it out all the time.

"We would budget, but sometimes, if you needed a pair of shoes and it wasn't in the budget, we would buy them.

That's the way it works when you have kids. But when the kids are older, you can budget a lot more, you know. We made sure you had three good meals and one good dress. We'd wash the dress instead of having a big wardrobe. You can't have a big wardrobe when you have five kids. Some people do that and they're broke all the time. They spend it on clothes, not necessities. Some kids were better dressed than you. We also bought things secondhand. It's better than paying high interest. The stuff still worked.

"I can't say it was tough raising five kids. Some had two kids and had a tougher time than we did. They had the same wages we did, but they bought more stuff for their kids. They spoiled their kids more. You really don't need to spoil kids that much, as long as they have the essentials. It doesn't matter if you have two or six kids, it's important to budget.

"Sometimes paying the bills was tough. We needed the RRSP money at times, but I never, ever touched that money. I had to put the bank loan on hold and I would communicate to the bank that when I sold my grain I would make that payment. They weren't always happy, but they knew they would get paid.

"I was always a budgeter. When I was in college I would get $10 a month. I had to make that last, so that's where I learned to budget. I always worked on a budget, even before I was married. I also worked Saturdays when I went to work in BC. I wanted to come back to Saskatchewan with some money and I did. If I'd been gallivanting every Saturday, like some of my friends did, I wouldn't be very far ahead. I did go out, but not every Saturday. Those Saturday wages paid for my fun. I didn't have to go into my week's wages. I wanted to save money to get 'married'. I was 22 years old when I got married.

"Buy a home. That's also an investment. Pay off your loans. A car loan is usually 10-12% interest or maybe even 20% interest. Buy a good second-hand car unless you can afford new. They'll both get you from A to B. New cars are okay if you can pay cash. Save to buy your car.

"Stay on the plus side. The minute you start paying interest, you're on the minus side. You have to add the pluses and the minuses. If you're in the plus, it's a good year. See where you're at. It's easy to manage and budget. Especially you guys. You know how much taxes you're going to pay. It was a lot harder for me. As a farmer you never knew 'til the end of the year where you were at. You never knew what you were going to get for your grain; you never knew how much grain you were going to sell, or when you'd be able to sell it. I went through that all my life. It wasn't easy to budget. Now it's easy to budget. I know where I'm at. I know how much I have and how much interest I'm making. When you know what you're making, it's easy to budget."

Save money

Never spend it

It's never too late

Start now.

To master money, you must manage money. It's not when I have it, I'll begin to manage it. It's when I begin to manage it, I'll have plenty of money.

Harv Ekker

Chapter Two:

GLOSSARY

This glossary will help you understand the financial terms used throughout the book.

What is the Golden Goose?

The Golden Goose is the money that you save on a monthly basis that you never, ever touch. It's your financial freedom account.

What are the Golden Eggs?

The Golden Eggs are the interest that you live on after years and years of savings.

What is an asset?

An asset is something you own that is of value.

What is a budget?

A budget is an estimate of income and expenditures for a set period of time.

What is overdraft protection?

Overdraft protection is an arrangement with a bank to have the ability to withdraw more that there is in the account, up to an agreed limit.

What is interest?

Interest is what you get paid for lending your money or what you pay for borrowing money.

What is compound interest?

Compound interest is when a person reinvests the interest, thus earning interest on top of interest.

What is financial freedom?

Financial freedom is the ability to live the lifestyle you desire without having to work or rely on anyone else for money.

What is passive income?

Passive income is money that is coming in without having to work. For example, the money you get from a renter or living off the interest you get from your Golden Goose.

What is a GIC (Guaranteed Investment Certificate)?

A GIC is an interest-paying investment in which the principal (your original contribution) and interest are guaranteed.

What is a Mutual Fund?

A mutual fund is an investment vehicle that can be compared to a basket full of stocks. You and many other investors pool your money to buy a portion of everything that's in the basket.

What is capital?

Capital is an investment available for producing more wealth. For example, the original money you invested in the RRSP is your capital.

What is an RRSP?

An RRSP is a registered retirement savings plan, which is a tax shelter to assist individuals in saving for their retirement.

What is risk tolerance?

Based on your investment decisions, risk tolerance is the point at which you can sleep at night and not have to worry about your investment.

What is a tax-free savings account?

A tax-free savings account is a registered account where the income earned in the account is tax-free, even when it is withdrawn. You can contribute up to $5,000 per year to a TFSA. The contributions you make are not deductible for income tax purposes.

What is the Rule of 72?

The rule of 72 tells you how long it will take for your money to double at different interest rates. 72 divided by the interest rate at which you are saving your money equals the amount of years it will take for you to double your money.

What is dollar cost averaging?

Dollar cost averaging is a technique used to lessen your investment risk, and is achieved when the same amount of money is invested regularly over a period of time (explained in chapter 4).

What is insurance?

Insurance is an arrangement by which a company provides a guarantee of compensation for specified loss, damage, illness, or death in return for payment of a premium.

What is a premium?

A premium is an amount to be paid for an insurance company.

What is a deductible?

A deductible is the amount you have to pay before the insurance policy kicks in. You will know this amount when you buy the insurance. You can decrease the cost of your insurance by increasing your deductible.

What is the time value of money?

The time value of money is simply the difference between a sum that is invested and the sum to which it will grow over time.

What is net/gross income?

Net income is the money that you are left with after all the deductions have been taken off your salary. Gross income is your salary before deductions.

What is credit rating?

Credit rating is a numeric ranking that indicates how credit-worthy previous lenders think you are. The rating is held in a report accessible through a credit bureau. It is updated every 30 days by those with whom you have lending agreements. Essentially, it is your financial reputation. It allows others, with whom you are making financial agreements, to review how you've dealt with your financial obligations in the past.

What is a creditor?

A Creditor is a person or company to whom you owe money to.

Without continuous learning, your life will not change. You must learn something today that will bring you another step closer to the success you desire.

Kevin Burns

Chapter Three:

THE REWARDS

In these chapters there are a lot of charts. Every chart has a different purpose. Whether these charts are compounding weekly, annually or anything in between is not important at this moment. Right now, the most important thing is that you have a visual to help you quickly understand the importance of creating your Golden Goose (Financial Freedom) account now.

The future value of money is greater than today's value because of interest earned on the money and the power of compounding. Compounding means money grows at a faster rate, since interest is earned on interest. Did you know that Albert Einstein called compound interest "the greatest mathematical discovery of all time"?

Learn the power of compounding through a game of golf:

Would you like to bet on a game of golf? How about if we bet 20 cents at the first hole and then double or nothing on the remaining 18 holes? If you are the more experienced golfer and you win at every hole, what do you stand to make? Dare to take a guess?

Enter your guess: _____

Here's how it works:

At the first hole, ... it's $.20

Second hole	$.40
Third hole	$ .80
Fourth hole	$1.60
Fifth hole	$3.20
Sixth hole	$6.40
Seventh hole	$12.80

Eighth hole	$25.60
Ninth hole	$51.20
Tenth hole	$102.40
Eleventh hole	$204.80
Twelfth hole	$409.60
Thirteenth hole	$819.20
Fourteenth hole	$1,638.40
Fifteenth hole	$3,276.80
Sixteenth hole	$6,553.60
Seventeenth hole	$13,107.20
Eighteenth hole	$26,214.40

Learn the power of compounding through a story:

A Grain of Rice and the Emperor's Daughter

The Chinese Emperor's daughter was ill, and so the Emperor promised riches beyond compare to whomever could cure her. Many tried and failed but a young peasant named Pong Lo, with his wit and bravery, restored the Princess' health and won her heart. As his reward, Pong Lo asked for her hand in marriage. The Emperor flatly refused, and asked the peasant to think of anything else he would like.

After several moments of thought, Pong Lo said, "I would like but one grain of rice."

"A grain of rice! That's nonsense! Ask me for fine silk, the grandest room in the palace, a stable full of wild stallions - ask and they will all be yours!"

"A grain of rice will do," said Pong Lo. "But if His Majesty insists, he may double the amount every day for a hundred days."

So on the first day a grain of rice was delivered to Pong Lo. On the second, two grains of rice were delivered. On the third day, Pong Lo received four grains, and on the fourth day, eight grains.

On the fifth day: 16 grains
On the sixth day: 32 grains
On the seventh day: 64 grains
On the eighth day: 128 grains

By the twelfth day, the grains of rice numbered 2,048. By the twentieth day, 524,288 grains were delivered. And by the thirtieth day, 536,870,912 grains – it required 40 servants to carry them to Pong Lo.

The Emperor realized what it would cost him if this continued and so in desperation he consented to the marriage. Out of consideration for the Emperor's feelings, no rice was served at the wedding banquet.

(Retold from *A Grain of Rice* by Helena Pittman; New York: Hastings House, 1986)

Learn how compounding differs when it's happening on a daily basis versus an annual basis:

Compound Interest Calculator
(money-zine.com)

Investment: $20,000
Interest Rate: 7%
Years: 5

	Interest Rate Compounded	Future Value Compounded
Daily	7.25	$28,380
Weekly	7.25	$28,375
Quarterly	7.23	$28,353
Semi-Annual	7.19	$28,212
Annual	7.12	$28,051

Learn the power of compounding through RRSPs as an investment vehicle:

We have more purchasing power if we use a tax deferred account; therefore, why not take advantage of an RRSP account to build your Golden Goose? Here is a quick sampling of the differences between investing in a **tax deferred** account versus a **taxed** account.

Compounded Growth Table

*$1200 invested annually **taxed** at a 30% tax rate*

10% interest	
5th yr	$7,384
10th yr	$17,740
15th yr	$32,266
20th yr	$52,638
25th yr	$81,212
30th yr	$121,288
35th yr	$177,496

Compounded Growth Table

$1200 invested annually **tax deferred**

10% interest	
5th yr	$8,059
10th yr	$21,037
15th yr	$41,940
20th yr	$75,603
25th yr	$129,818
30th yr	$217,132
35th yr	$357,752

Learn how $1000 grows, even if you don't add another penny.

Compounded Growth Table

$1000 invested at 10% interest

1st yr	$1,100
5th yr	$1,611
10th yr	$2,594
15th yr	$4,177
20th yr	$6,727
25th yr	$10,835
30th yr	$17,449
35th yr	$28,102
40th yr	$45,259
50th yr	$117,391
100th yr	$13,780,612
200th yr	$189,905,276,460

Would this help create a legacy for your family or others? Would you have the freedom to live the life you were truly meant to live?

Would you be able to accomplish a few big dreams? Would you be able to spend more time with the ones you love?

Would you have the power to determine where you can spend your time?

Would you have the ability to donate your time or money to an organization that you truly believe in?

Would you feel alive and full of energy?

Would you be happy, knowing that you have the means to help make this world a better place?

Are you ready to commit and persevere?

Are you up for the challenge?

For every dollar you receive, you have two choices. You can spend it or you can save it. Spend it and it's gone forever, save it and you'll have it forever... and you can spend what it produces.

George S. Clason

Chapter Four:

IT'S THAT EASY

Pay Yourself First

This concept can't be stressed enough. We usually pay for our entertainment and our bills first, and then we're left with nothing at the end of the month to save. Make a point of feeding the Golden Goose first. Then proceed with paying off the rest of your bills. Deposit an amount you can afford and then, as you earn more or your financial situation changes to the good, increase that amount.

Consider Dollar Cost Averaging

Investing a sum of money each month into an investment where dollar cost averaging is permitted, greatly reduces your risk. Let me show you how it works.

Invest $100 per month in company shares.

Month	Dollar invested	Price/share	# of shares purchased
1	$100	$10	10
2	$100	$5	20
3	$100	$10	10

By the end of month three, you own forty shares. If the price of the share had remained constant, your $100 would have purchased only ten shares per month and the total number of shares that you would own is 30 shares, not 40 like the example above.

The lesson to learn here is that, even if the price per share goes down, you are buying a greater number of shares. So a declining price of the share is not bad news if you can be patient and only sell when the price of the shares is higher than what you paid for the shares.

The clock is ticking. Pay yourself first today.

Start Young

Although students and young adults may not feel they have much in the way of assets, the greatest asset they have is TIME.

Example one:

In this example, Sue saves $100 a month for the first 15 years and never puts another penny in the account. Jill waits 15 years and then invests $100 per month for the next 25 years. Who is further ahead? What's your guess? This example uses a 10% return.

Year	Save (Sue)	Save (Jill)
1	$1200	0
2	$1200	0
3	$1200	0
4	$1200	0
5	$1200	0
6	$1200	0
7	$1200	0
8	$1200	0
9	$1200	0
10	$1200	0
11	$1200	0
12	$1200	0
13	$1200	0
14	$1200	0
15	$1200	0
16	0	$1200
17	0	$1200
18	0	$1200
19	0	$1200
20	0	$1200

Year	Save (Sue)	Save (Jill)
21	0	$1200
22	0	$1200
23	0	$1200
24	0	$1200
25	0	$1200
26	0	$1200
27	0	$1200
28	0	$1200
29	0	$1200
30	0	$1200
31	0	$1200
32	0	$1200
33	0	$1200
34	0	$1200
35	0	$1200
36	0	$1200
37	0	$1200
38	0	$1200
39	0	$1200
40	0	$1200
Contribution	**$18,000**	**$30,000**
Golden Goose	**$431,702**	**$123,332**

As you can see, even though Jill invested $12,000 more and over a longer period, Sue has more money in her Golden Goose account because she started sooner. TIME is your greatest asset.

Let me stress this point again. For the young and wise who realize the value of time, the Golden Goose is the key to living the life of your dreams.

Example two: Find your age. This is how much you will need to save each month to have $1,000,000 (one million dollars) at age 65, assuming a 10% return.

Age	Monthly	Age	Monthly
1	$14	16	$64
2	$16	17	$71
3	$17	18	$78
4	$19	19	$86
5	$21	20	$95
6	$23	21	$106
7	$26	22	$117
8	$29	23	$129
9	$32	24	$143
10	$35	25	$158
11	$39	26	$175
12	$43	27	$194
13	$47	28	$215
14	$52	29	$238
15	$58	30	$263

What if you were 35? You would need $442/month. What if you were 40? You would need $754/month. What if you were 45? You would need $1317/month.

Now, if you want to have some fun figuring it out for yourself, get on the Internet and Google: compound interest monthly calculator. Fill in the blanks.

Some of you might need less of a Golden Goose. Work out your numbers. How fat do you want your Golden Goose to be? Everybody's needs will be different.

Make Your Financial Plan Automatic

Building your Golden Goose automatically is the one step that guarantees you won't fail. Ask your employer to debit a portion of each pay cheque into a savings/RRSP account or arrange for the bank to make an automatic withdrawal for you. The plan, once set up, allows you to go about your life and not spend a lot of time thinking or worrying about your money. Why is this important?

It's important because what's missing in our lives today is time. Make your financial plan automatic and one of the powerful things you will get back is worry-free time.

The book you don't read won't help.

Jim Rohn

Chapter Five:

WHO HAS THE POWER?

Are You in Control?

A faucet dripping once per second can release 50 gallons of water in one week. A slow trickle of money can gradually fill financial reservoirs, or drain them dry.

Just one dollar a day can have tremendous impact over a 45-year career, depending on whether it is saved (filling your reservoir) or added to debt (draining your reservoir).

The chart on this page compares the value of saving a dollar per day in a cookie jar, in a mutual fund RRSP earning 10% interest, or charged to a credit card with a 20% interest rate.

Years	Cookie Jar	RRSP mutual fund earning 10%	Charged to a credit card at 20%
5	$1,825	$2,329	-$2,957
10	$3,650	$6,080	-$10,316
15	$5,475	$12,121	-$28,626
20	$7,300	$21,849	-$74,190
25	$9,125	$37,518	-$187,566
30	$10,950	$62,752	-$469,681
35	$12,775	$103,391	-$1,171,674
40	$14,600	$168,842	-$2,918,457
45	$16,425	$274,250	-$7,265,012

Are you in control of your money?

OR

Is your debt controlling you?

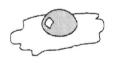

Major Purchases

Why do so many of us live backwards in our financial lives? We spend first (using a credit card) and then slowly and painfully, we pay off our credit card. We get the new furniture now and by the time we pay off the credit card, we've spent twice the originally cost. Let's consider the purchase of a car:

A $20,000 car can cost as little as $17,700 or as much as $25,500 depending on whether we save for it in advance or incur debt to purchase it now.

Save First	Take out a Loan
Save $20,000 and then buy	Borrow $20,000 and buy now
It takes you 5 years to save	It takes you 5 years to pay off the loan
Your savings account earns 5% interest	Your cost of borrowing is 10% interest
Monthly saving $295	Monthly payment $425
Total Payments 60 (12 months x 5 yrs.)	Total Payments 60 (12 months x 5yrs)
My cost $17,700 thanks to compound interest	My cost $25,500
You save $2,300 ($20,000-$17,000)	**You lose $7,800 ($25,500-17,700)**

Many Canadians sliding deeper into debt

Delayed Gratification

Do you buy the item now and temporarily feel the excitement of your new purchase? Or do you wait until you have the cash to buy the item, save mega dollars on interest charges, and forever enjoy the item knowing that you've made a wise purchase? And where does your savings go? Hopefully into your Golden Goose account.

Delayed gratification is about buying items at a later time. Like when we can afford them or when we have saved for the items. We need to evaluate all of our purchases. Waiting to have the money to buy the things we need or want will be less stressful in the long run.

In the future, ask yourself if your purchase is a need or want. Sometimes, it may be wise to purchase our needs and not our wants. Another tactic might be to wait a week before deciding whether or not to make the purchase. We may realize that, that purchase is not important after all. Make wise choices and stay within your budget guidelines.

Savings on Additional Payments

On a $100,000 home loan for thirty years at 7% interest, your monthly payment would be $665 a month and the final cost of the loan would be more than double what you borrowed. However, paying just a little extra every month could dramatically reduce the total cost of the loan and the length of your debt.

Extra Payment	Out of Debt	Total Interest
0	30 years	$139,511
$25/mth	< 27 years	$121,296
$50/mth	< 24 years	$107,856
$100/mth	< 21 years	$89,003

Even making bi-weekly (every two weeks) payment on your mortgage will dramatically reduce the amount of interest you'll have to pay. Why? Because you end up making two additional payments each year. Don't let the bank decide what your mortgage payment will be. They tend to estimate low. That's to their advantage because they will earn more interest from you in the long run. Pay as much as you can afford to pay while staying within your budget.

... worries about money may mock you. They steal the joy of living because they follow you around all day like a dark menacing shadow. At night they hover at the foot of your bed, waiting to rob you of sleep. When you're worried about money you dread the days and you agonize at night. Without thinking, you throw away every precious twenty-four hours that comes your way. You cease to live and merely exist.

Sarah Ban Breathnach:
Simple Abundance

Chapter Six:

THE GRIM REALITY....
IT'S NOT TOO LATE

If You Lose, Don't Lose the Lesson

Dad told me in my early 20s that I needed to save money and never, ever spend that money, so that it could grow. You go to school, you get married, you have a family and life takes over. And then one day you wake up and 25 years have gone by. That's why Dad's wisdom is so important to me now, and even more so to his grandchildren - because time is on their side.

Am I growing my Golden Goose? Yes, but not as early as I would have liked. Had I listened to the wisdom of my dad back when

I was 20 and fed my Golden Goose $100 per month, I would be well on my way to financial freedom with $345,493 in my account.

I work towards accelerating the growth of my Golden Goose. I continue to educate myself so that I can make wise decisions.

Never stop learning. Bit by bit, you will understand more and, in the end, make better decisions. Pensions at work are a great way to create your Golden Goose. For those who don't have a pension, it's even more crucial to open an RRSP and get started on your Golden Goose account now.

Beliefs of the Broke versus the Rich

Broke people believe the primary reason to work is to earn money to pay for their current lifestyle. Rich people believe the primary reason to work is to earn money to invest and to create passive income structures so they can win the money game and be financially free.

What do you believe?

The Grim Reality

Household debt is on the increase, jeopardize-ing the average person's financial security.

What I am hearing and reading is that:

- many lines of credit are maxed out

- many are living from pay cheque to pay cheque

- many are in over their heads and can no longer manage their debt load.

- many wished they'd have received more financial training at school

Having the knowledge, skills and confidence to make responsible financial decisions is essential for basic functioning. Daily we are confronted with financial decisions that can have significant consequences on our future.

Is it too Late?

It's never too late to improve your financial situation. If you do not belong to a workplace pension plan, start accumulating preretirement savings, through an RRSP.

Awareness and action are key.
Begin the process now:
- Let go of the past; you can't change it.
- There is no such thing as failure if you learn from it.
- Spend less than you make.
- Simplify.
- Find other ways to increase your income
- Pay yourself first.

Start now

Never regret. If it's good, it's wonderful. If it's bad, it's experience.

Victoria Holt

Chapter Seven:

WINNING AT
THE MONEY GAME

In order to achieve financial freedom, you need to consistently apply this simple formula:

- SPEND less than you make.

- INVEST the difference.

- REINVEST your returns (compound interest).

This formula will ensure that there will come a day when you never, ever have to work again, or that if you do work, it's because you want to.

Winning at the money game is feeding the goose consistently so that she eventually produces an abundance of eggs to pay for the lifestyle you desire. When your supply of eggs exceeds your expenses, you will be financially free.

To figure out approximately how much money it will take for you to retire and live the lifestyle you want, follow these directions:

Step one:

Write down the total amount of money you think you will need per year to live on:

_____=A (net income)

For example, Joe needs $70,000 per year to live the lifestyle he wants.

Step two:

Add 50% to cover inflation and taxes:

A + A/2 = _____ =B (gross income)

For example, Joe will add 50 percent of $70,000 to his initial figure to account for taxes and inflation. He now knows he needs $105,000 per year ($70,000 + $70, 000/2).

Step three:

If you expect to have a 10% return on your investment, multiply your gross income (B) x 10 to see how much money you will need working for you.

B _____ x 10 = _____ =C (Golden Goose)

For example, Joe is expecting a 10% return on his investment so he will need to build his Golden Goose to $1,050,000. ($105,000 x 10 = $1,050,000)

In other words, when Joe's Golden Goose account is worth $1,050,000 and it is earning 10% interest, it will produce golden eggs (passive income) worth $105,000 per year.

$1,050,000.00 $105,000.00

Keep feeding the Goose and never, ever spend the Golden Goose (Financial Freedom) account. When the Goose is nice and fat, you can live off the Golden Eggs (interest).

Will $1,000,000 (one million dollars) in your Golden Goose account meet your needs?

Take into account that we generally need less of an income during retirement years. You will probably have your mortgage paid off, and your life insurance premiums may be reduced or disappear entirely. Clothing for work and daily transportation will not be an issue. Your children will no longer be living at home, so this should greatly reduce your grocery bill and other expenses.

Everyone's Golden Goose needs are going to be different. That's why it's so important to set goals and know how much money it will take for you to achieve these goals. As they say, if you fail to plan, you plan to fail.

If you don't know where you're going, how are you going to get there?

You miss 100% of the shots you don't take.

Wayne Gretzky

Chapter Eight:

NEW CHOICES

Do I still have your attention? Is building the Golden Goose something that you want to do? Do you still feel like you have no money to contribute, but you desperately want to? Take a look at these new choices that may help you on your road to freedom.

Financial

1. Pay off your credit card monthly and avoid paying fees.

2. Pay off your mortgage early (Bi-weekly payments, lumps sums, increase your payment).

3. Pay your bills on time to avoid late fees. Talk to your creditors. They may forgo the penalty if you are only a few days late in making your payment.

4. If you get a raise, add to your Golden Goose (Financial Freedom Account) and/or pay off debt.

5. Review your statements for accuracy. Mistakes can be costly.

6. Consider getting a no-fee bank account and benefit from free cheques and no-fee banking.

7. Use your free cheques instead of using e-transfer and save on service charges.

8. Avoid fees by withdrawing cash from your personal bank's ATM machines.

10. Budget so you can avoid going into your overdraft and paying overdraft charges. Overdraft is for emergencies and should not be a regular occurrence.

11. Establish a good credit history by paying your bills on time, and enjoy lower interest rates.

Transportation

1. Buy a pre-owned car.

2. Carpool.

3. Find the lowest gas prices.

4. Save for your car and pay cash for it.

Food

1. Bring lunches to work.

2. Bring snacks and drinks to avoid using vending machines.

3. Eat leftovers.

4. Shop with a list. Avoid purchases that are not on your list.

5. Make your own coffee.

6. Drink water at restaurants.

7. Eat your snack before going to the movies.

8. Buy store-brand items.

Travel and vacations

1. Travel off season.

2. Use discount travel websites.

3. Travel with friends for group rates.

4. Join a frequent flyer reward program.

5. Share a hotel room at hockey tournaments.

6. Drive within the speed limit. This saves on speeding tickets and gas.

Insurance

1. Know your work insurance plan to avoid duplication at home.

2. Drive an older car. It's cheaper on insurance.

3. Decrease your insurance expense by increasing your deductible (evaluate the pro and cons before deciding).

4. Shop around for lower rates.

Taxes

1. Start a home-based business and save on taxes.

2. Donate and save on taxes. Bring your receipts to your accountant.

Utilities

1. Turn off the lights when you leave the room.

2. Use a fan instead of the air conditioner.

3. Use a power bar for your equipment and power it off, when not in use.

4. Wear a sweater instead of turning up the heat.

5. Dry your clothes on a clothesline.

6. Review your phone and internet plan to ensure they meet your needs in the most cost effective way.

7. Change your cable TV to a basic program, or cancel it.

Other

1. Get a library card and save on books and movies.

2. Purchase magazine subscriptions rather than buying them at the newsstand.

3. Buy clothes that don't need to be dry-cleaned.

4. Watch movies at home.

5. Move in with family and share the expenses.

6. Use coupons and watch for sales.

7. Bring your bottles to the depot for a refund.

8. Work overtime or get a part time job.

9. Have a garage sale.

10. Rent out a room in your home.

What new choices will you make? What are some other ways you can save money?

Be Creative

When my daughter was in grade 10, she had the opportunity to go on a school trip to Quebec. The cost was $1,200. I did not have $1,200 at the time but I told her we would find a way to pay for the trip. We were already delivering telephone books for one of her hockey fundraisers. The manager agreed to let us do two extra routes. We also tried filling sandbags one afternoon. Her brother came to help. We were constantly changing our approach to filling the sandbags so that we were finally working for a decent wage. We were in the fresh air, getting exercise, spending quality time with family and having a few good laughs. Finally, I found her a babysitting job. A five-year-old from her school would get on the bus with her and she would watch her till 5:30, Monday to Friday. My daughter managed to earn $1,000 of the $1,200 for that trip. Involve the kids and make it a family affair. Not only will the relationships blossom, you are also teaching your kids that there is always a way to make your dreams come true, if you are willing to put in the work.

What are some ideas you can come up with for your kids to help pay for some of their expenses? Have you thought of a paper route?

What are some ideas you can come up with for yourself?

The Choices that We Make Every Day

Stop spending your hard-earned dollars on things that aren't really important to you. Save those dollars for things that will bring you pleasure. When evaluating your options, consider how much it will cost you over the year. Once you've figured that out, decide whether or not you still want to buy it.

For example:

One $4 magazine per month is $48 per year

One $10 pack of cigarettes per day is $300 per month or $3,650 per year

One $7 Subway meal per week is $364 per year

One $2 cup of coffee per day is $730 per year

Low-cost simple pleasures

Laughing so hard your face hurts

Shopping when there are no lineups

Going for a nature walk

Getting a letter in the mail

Taking a drive on a country road

Listening to your favorite songs

Getting a hug from a child

Doing an act of kindness for a stranger

Eating your favorite ice cream

Relaxing in a warm bath

Feeling the pride of getting things done

Finding a $20 bill in your coat

Catching a fish

Connecting with friends and family

Going for a run

Swinging on a swing

Playing hockey on an outdoor rink

Watching the sunrise or sunset

Reflecting on what is good in your life

Sleighing with a flattened box

Making snow angels

Underwrite your life. Be accountable and responsible and don't point the finger at anyone but yourself.

Kevin Burns

Chapter Nine:

THE MAGIC OF GIVING

Do you remember the last time you gave someone a gift?

How did that make you feel?

Do you remember the last time you gave of your time to someone or something you believed in?

How did that make you feel?

Giving is a joyful, wonderful experience.

Give More, Live More

Money can make your life easier but it won't always bring you happiness. Real happiness comes from within. It comes from living a life of meaning. Having a higher purpose than just making a lot of money is critical for long-term happiness and personal fulfillment.

Make a difference in people's lives and give more. The more you give, the more fully alive you will feel. It is so rewarding.

Universal Truth

The one universal truth that has stood the test of time is that the more you give, the more you receive. If you are looking to attract more wealth and happiness into your life, try giving. Donate money to a nonprofit organization or give of your time.

As I continue to study, I've noticed that the people who achieve great wealth have at least one thing in common - giving.

Does giving away money really attract more money?

Try it and see what happens.

Learn to Receive

Giving is easy and we love to do it because it makes us feel great. But, receiving is not so easy. I speak from experience - it took me many years to grasp this concept. You know how good it makes you feel when you give something to someone. When you don't accept the gift given to you, you are robbing that person of that wonderful opportunity to feel great. It is actually a very selfish act. When I finally connected with this concept, my life changed. When someone gives me something now, I think of it as a blessing. I say thank you, and I watch the giver beam with joy.

Tithing

Tithing is giving a portion of the money that comes into your life back out to help others. I've learnt that service always comes before rewards. As we make a difference in the world, differences will occur in our own life.

How much should I give?

It is recommended you give 10% of your income.

Where should I give?

Give toward something that you believe in - something that is working toward a greater good for our world - and feel good that you are part of making a difference.

Last but not least, make it automatic so you really don't have to think about it.

We make a living by what we earn - we make a life by what we give.

Winston Churchill

Chapter Ten:

IMPORTANCE OF BUDGETING

Many people have no idea how much they earn or spend per month. *The consequence of not knowing is debt.* That is why budgeting is so important. If you want to get out of debt, it is important to know how much money you bring in per month and where that money is going.

How to come up with your budget

Keep track of absolutely everything you spend in a month. Do this for one month but for a more accurate picture keep track for three months. Ask for a receipt for all of your purchases. Nightly or weekly, enter your amounts into an Excel table that you create (or find on google) or simply use something similar to the next table.

You will want to decide on your categories. They can be general (utilities) or detailed (phone, gas, electricity).

Month of _____			Total
Income	200,1500,1000	2700	
Total Income			**2700**
Utilities	50,75,125,100,	350	
Insurance	80, 82, 40	202	
Transportatio n	10, 40, 42	92	
Mortgage/rent	905	905	
Groceries	10, 60, 140, 200	410	
GoldenGoose (Savings)	100	100	
Emergency fund	80	80	

Health	10, 50, 20	80	
Donation	20, 100, 40, 100	260	
Household	80, 10, 10	100	
Entertainment	40, 30, 10	80	
	Total Expenses	**2659**	

Other categories may include: subscriptions, childcare, gifts, travel, income tax, professional fees, etc.

After three months you should have a really good idea as to where your money is going and what it is costing you to live.

Don't forget to include yearly expenses. For example your tax bill may be $1200/year. In order to include that amount on your monthly budget sheet, just divide it by 12. Under household you would add $10 per month to budget for that expense.

Don't stop there

If you are really serious about eliminating debt and getting ahead, keep track monthly.

Is it a need or a want?

Evaluate all of your purchases. Do I need it or do I want it?

If you need it, and you can afford it, purchase it.

If it is a want, wait a day or two before making the purchase. You may decide that it is not important to purchase this item after all. Also, ask yourself if this item is low or high on your priority list. Focus on items that are high on you priority list. If it is really important for you to have this item, brainstorm new, positive ways to come up with the money.

Good debt and bad debt

Good debt: Borrowing money to build wealth is basically what a good debt is all about. In the long term a good debt will increase your net worth. Examples of a good debt are: mortgages, rental properties, new businesses. It can also be as simple as borrowing money for adding insulation in your attic which ultimately will save you on your utilities bill.

Bad debt: On the contrary, bad debt is borrowed money that does not increase wealth. This would include non-essential items, luxuries, paying high interest on credit cards, etc.

Christmas, birthdays..

Going into debt to buy presents is not a good idea. Only buy what you can afford. My Christmas budget changes every year. This year, as a family, we decided that we would not buy each other presents. Being together is what we valued. In the past we have done Chinese gift exchanges or picked names.

Be creative. There are many thoughtful gestures that are worth more than anything money can buy. Here are a few ideas: quality time, a beautiful card with a personal message from your heart, an offer to babysit or cook a meal, homemade salsa, pool passes for an outing together.

Are you saving for a rainy day?

An emergency fund is a great way to save for a rainy day. Life is full of uncertainties (loss of a job, sickness, and family emergencies). Having three months' worth of wages in your emergency fund can relieve a lot of stress. Add monthly to this fund. Make it a mandatory category.

Discretionary vs. Mandatory expenses

Discretionary expenses: expenses that we do not need to make. (e.g. latte, entertainment, magazine subscriptions)

Mandatory expenses: expenses that we need to make. (e.g. rent, utilities, savings, emergency fund)

Create your budget sheet and take the time to notice if your expense categories are discretionary or mandatory.

Benefits of Budgeting

- You will eventually be in control of your money instead of debt controlling you
- Your stress will decrease
- You will know where your money is going
- You will know what it costs you to live
- You will know what you can afford
- You will know where to cut back
- You will be able to accelerate paying off your debts
- You will be able to add to your savings

The consequence of not budgeting is debt. The advantage of budgeting is that eventually you will pay off your debt and when you pay off your debt, it will be like winning a lottery. Now, we could all use the feeling of winning a lottery; and, unlike other lotteries, the odds are in your favor.

If you manage your money, you will have more; if you don't manage your money you won't have any.

People commonly make the mistake of spending money on smaller items which are low on their priority list and, as a result, cannot afford the big things high on their list.

The Tightwad Gazette

Chapter Eleven:

GET ON BOARD

Anybody can take action; you just need a strong enough reason why. Putting this book together was fun, challenging and surprisingly quick. Why was I so motivated to write this book, and why was I able to accomplish my goal so fast? It's simple. My "why" was huge. Dad's birthday was coming up, and I wanted to give him this book as a thank you for all the times that he gently offered his advice. My other big reason is that the clock is ticking. I want to get this information out to as many people as possible, as quickly as I can, so that you are inspired to begin working toward your own financial freedom.

If you need to get yourself motivated to act, find a strong reason why financial freedom is important to you. Once you decide what that reason is, it's important to take action immediately toward that goal. Never leave the site of a decision without initiating action, regardless of how small the action is. Even if it's just writing yourself a note to call the bank tomorrow, to set up an appointment, do something. Take some sort of action, and continue to take action one step at a time. So take a few minutes and decide.

Why is financial freedom important to you?

Is it to have the freedom to build a legacy for your loved ones?

Is it to have the freedom to live your passion? To live the life you were meant to live?

Is it to have the freedom to accomplish all the things on your bucket list?

Is it to have the freedom to change something for the better?

Is it to have the freedom to care for those you love?

Be specific. Find a reason that really gets you excited. A reason that makes you feel alive and full of life. A reason that will keep you up late at night or get you out of bed early in the morning juiced about setting your goals for the day.

Where Do I Start?

- ❏ Create a budget.
- ❏ Make the commitment to pay yourself first.
- ❏ Commit to never spend your Golden Goose Account.
- ❏ Automate your savings.
- ❏ Spend less than you make.
- ❏ Sign up for your retirement plan at work.
- ❏ Open an RRSP account.
- ❏ Consider funding a Tax Free Savings Account.
- ❏ Know your interest rates. Read the fine print.
- ❏ Make a plan to pay off your debts.
- ❏ Pay off your credit cards monthly.

- Maintain good communication with your creditors.
- Negotiate lower interest rates on your borrowed accounts.
- Get a second job.
- Work toward owning a home.
- Figure out how much you will need to retire (ch.7).
- Make sure you have basic life insurance coverage (car, home, life).
- Open a no-fee bank account and get free cheques.
- Start a home-based business and save on taxes.
- Never stop learning. Read 10 minutes a day or more.
- Find something to be grateful for each and every day.
- Donate to a cause that you believe in.
- Teach your loved ones to feed their Golden Goose.
- Pinpoint your "why" for wanting to get ahead.
- Pick an action item to work on today.

On a Final Note

If you keep doing what you've always done, you'll keep getting what you always got. Can you see that keeping up with the Joneses is leading you into a financial trap?

I hope that, by reading this book, you have grasped the value of time and the importance of building your Golden Goose account now.

Take action now, and review your accomplishments every three to six months. No matter how slowly you seem to be moving, be proud and celebrate. Never stop learning. Read financial books. Find mentors. Ask questions. Google financial terms that you don't understand.

Slowly you will learn more; and, the more you learn, the wiser your choices are going to be. Are you up for the challenge? Are you willing to commit and persevere on this quest to financial freedom? This is your future we're talking about.

I believe that you were meant to read this book. I believe that you are on this planet for a reason. I believe you were born with unique gifts, talents and dreams. And my experience has taught me that financial challenges are what holds most people back from their purpose in life.

Break the financial handcuffs of living from pay cheque to pay cheque. Regain control and notice your financial worries disappear. It's time to focus on what is most important to you.

How? Start by committing to one important step to financial freedom:

Create your Golden Goose Account. Never, ever spend it and start producing those Golden Eggs.

If you would like more copies of this book please visit:
www.suzannejubb.com

The major reason for setting a goal is for what it makes of you to accomplish it. What it makes of you will always be far greater value than what you get.

Jim Rohn

A Journal:
Questions that really matter...
a pathway to happiness

This journal was created to help you reflect on the things that really matter in life. It will also help you clarify what you really want and why you want it. If you don't take the time to do so, you will find yourself reacting to everyone else's demands. There are many gold nuggets in this book that will inspire you to move towards a more balanced life.

It is a journal that you will want to revisit often.

Journal will launch in April 2016

About The Author

Suzanne is presently working as a community and program facilitator, but her true passion is teaching.

She has been teaching for well over 30 years in different capacities. Her gift is her ability to simplify the material so that all learners can benefit from the learning experience.

She strives to continually improve in all areas of life and not a day goes by where she is not learning.

Suzanne is passionate about helping others.

Connect with Suzanne on her website:
www.suzannejubb.com

Made in the USA
Middletown, DE
12 February 2016